W9-AAK-646
Oracle Press™

Grid Revolution:
An Introduction to
Enterprise Grid Computing

Brajesh Goyal
Shilpa Lawande

McGraw-Hill/Osborne

New York Chicago San Francisco
Lisbon London Madrid Mexico City Milan
New Delhi San Juan Seoul Singapore Sydney Toronto

The *McGraw-Hill* Companies

McGraw-Hill/Osborne
2100 Powell Street, 10th Floor
Emeryville, California 94608
U.S.A.

To arrange bulk purchase discounts for sales promotions, premiums, or
fund-raisers, please contact **McGraw-Hill/Osborne** at the above address.
For information on translations or book distributors outside the U.S.A.

Grid Revolution: An Introduction to Enterprise Grid Computing

234567890 CUS CUS 019876

ISBN 0-07-226281-8

Acquisitions Editor	Lisa McClain
Project Editor	Mark Karmendy
Acquisitions Coordinator	Alex McDonald
Technical Editors	Bob Thome, Miranda Nash, & Moe Fardoost
Copy Editor	Mark Karmendy
Proofreader	Susie Elkind
Indexer	Claire Splan
Composition	Apollo Publishing Services
Series Design	Jean Butterfield
Cover Designer	Damore Johann Design, Inc.

This book was composed with Corel VENTURA™ Publisher.

About the Authors

Brajesh Goyal is the senior manager for database solutions and grid computing at Network Appliance. He is leading Network Appliance's strategy and efforts for delivering storage grid solutions for business applications and databases. Before NetApp, Brajesh was the principal product manager for grid computing at Oracle, where he was among the first few people to explore grid computing and influence Oracle's strategy and efforts in the grid space. Brajesh has an MS in Computer Science from University of Minnesota, Minneapolis, and a B.Tech in Computer Science from Indian Institute of Technology, Mumbai.

Shilpa Lawande has several years of experience with Oracle database technology and products. During her tenure at Oracle, she worked on various aspects of Oracle's data warehousing and self-managing technologies. Shilpa has co-authored two books—*Oracle 9iR2 Data Warehousing* (Digital Press, 2003) and *Oracle 10g Data Warehousing* (Digital Press, 2004). She has an MS in Computer Science from University of Wisconsin-Madison and a B.Tech. in Computer Science from Indian Institute of Technology, Mumbai. Shilpa currently works for a Boston-area data warehousing startup.

CONTENTS

ACKNOWLEDGMENTS

We would like to profusely thank all our reviewers, especially Bob Thome, Miranda Nash, Pankhuri Agrawal, and Moe Fardoost. Their diligent review and hard work helped us in substantially improving the quality of the book and conveying the messages more crisply.

We would also like to thank Lisa McClain and the team at Oracle Press for their support in the production of the book.

INTRODUCTION

The book provides an introduction to enterprise grid computing and its application to an Oracle environment. It starts with a discussion of the business demands of IT today and the challenges faced by enterprises attempting to meet these demands. It describes how enterprise grid computing can help in addressing these challenges. The authors follow the evolution of enterprise grid computing from its origin in scientific and technical computing to the current state of the art, and then provide a future roadmap. The book also gives a brief overview of the grid standards landscape. It concludes with a discussion on practical steps to transition an existing enterprise IT architecture towards an enterprise grid, while gaining significant grid computing benefits along the way.

1

Motivation for Enterprise Grid Computing

With the advent of e-business in the 1990s, Information Technology (IT) has taken center stage in the operation of business. Every successful business now has an online presence, which must be backed up by a solid IT department, either in-house or outsourced. IT departments are constantly driven to deliver more capabilities and higher quality of service to the end users. Traditionally, this meant deploying systems with better performance and availability, which translated to fast and reliable processing of user requests. During good economic times, enterprises would try to achieve any shortcomings by investing heavily in IT infrastructure and personnel. However, in the current economic climate, enterprises are forced to be more careful with their operating expenses and return on investment (ROI). As IT budgets have shrunk dramatically, IT executives are trying to achieve the same quality of service by improving overall efficiency of IT and business processes and via better automation. Further, enterprises are now looking to differentiate themselves by being able to quickly and constantly adapt their business processes to meet changing market needs. In a nutshell, the goal enterprises are seeking today is efficiency of business processes, aided by a flexible and yet cost-effective IT infrastructure.

Unfortunately, it is becoming apparent that currently deployed IT infrastructure is not quite suited to achieve these goals. The fundamental reason for this is the ad-hoc manner in which enterprise IT architectures have evolved. The well-intentioned effort towards bigger and faster IT systems has, over the years, resulted in many monolithic silos of computing infrastructure within a single enterprise. While some systems are unable to cope with increased loads, many others are heavily underutilized. As isolated islands of infrastructure, it is not easy to shuffle these systems around to utilize them as necessary. The same is true at the business applications front, where business logic and process workflows are hardwired within monolithic applications. Information used by various business applications lies fragmented in numerous databases and legacy systems, unable to be shared.

Enterprise grid computing is a new model for enterprise computing, which offers a path forward from the current state of enterprise IT. It allows enterprises to incrementally evolve their IT architecture while leveraging existing assets and investments. Before we delve into the workings of Enterprise grid computing, let us take a closer look at the business demands today and analyze issues with currently deployed IT architectures.

Business Demands Today

As we discussed in the introduction, enterprises today are looking for ways to differentiate themselves via better and more efficient business processes. With an unfavorable economy, throwing money at the problem is not a sustainable approach. Therefore, fundamentally, there are two requirements for business applications and the underlying IT infrastructure: (a) provide flexibility to meet changing business demands and (b) deliver value for money.

Flexibility and Responsiveness to Business Demands

Enterprises constantly seek to improve quality of service delivered to customers and end users. With the ubiquity of the Internet, the number of user requests that must be supported—and hence the underlying computational needs of the enterprise—have grown to unprecedented levels. A breaking news story or a sale of a hot item can suddenly draw millions of users to the enterprise web site. In this situation, a slow web site can result in the loss of a loyal customer to a competitor. The IT department must be able to quickly marshal the necessary computational resources to handle this surge in demand to deliver a predictable quality of service to the end user. Similarly, downtime of a critical system can result in lost productivity, lost revenue, lost customer goodwill, bad press, and lawsuits. The IT department must provide resilient infrastructure to handle such failures.

Enterprises today are always on the edge and looking for opportunities to secure and expand their business. Flexibility in business operations has become a necessity for survival. Unfortunately today, there are long IT lead times to deploying new products and services. It may take many days or months before IT can handle the needs of a new application or business process, and it often means going through the entire process of acquiring and building systems from the ground up. Frequently, the information a company needs to run the business and make decisions is either unobtainable or difficult to get to quickly when and where it is needed. Business process flows are hardwired and not amenable to change.

Enterprises would like to have an IT infrastructure that can realign itself expeditiously to new business priorities. They require rapid and predictable turnaround times for provisioning requests for computing power, storage, information, and application flows.

Better Value for Money

During the Y2K crisis and the dotcom boom, spending on IT infrastructure and IT-related business initiatives went through the roof, without necessarily delivering returns. This has led to some disenchantment with IT and caused a perception that IT is a costly overhead to the business. The result is that IT expenditure is now more thoroughly scrutinized. For the past three or four years, IT executives have been under severe pressure to reduce overall costs and deliver ROI on ongoing projects.

Necessity is the mother of invention. The need to reduce costs has led IT executives to take a hard look at how IT is being done today, from the point of view of both technology and processes. One of the ways to lower the costs of IT infrastructure is to better utilize currently deployed hardware, software, and administrative resources and to reduce the ongoing cost of application development, deployment, and maintenance. Another approach is to simplify the operation and management of IT systems so that existing IT staff can scale to manage more systems more efficiently, thereby reducing overall costs. It is also becoming crucial to monitor IT systems with respect to various metrics such as utilization, reliability, and performance, so that IT executives can justify additional spending when truly required.

An efficient, cost-effective, and agile IT and business process infrastructure can truly be a competitive asset to the enterprise. However, IT departments today find it extremely difficult to achieve these goals. To understand why, it is necessary to take a closer look at current IT system deployments and understand the issues with them.

Enterprise IT Architecture Today

Enterprises typically consist of several autonomous business units, each with varying business objectives. Over the years, as each business unit independently tries to deliver the required functionality and quality of service to its users, it inadvertently creates silos of applications and IT systems infrastructure. This results in the emergence of islands of information and computing infrastructure within a single enterprise. These islands are unable to communicate or share resources with each other. The resulting picture is demonstrated by Figure 1-1.

Each silo consists of several components, including hardware, software, business applications, databases, and other legacy information systems. Each business unit typically has its own staff of system administrators who manage the systems. The IT systems are further complicated by stove-piped solutions for operational elements such as security and high availability. Figure 1-1 only depicts the tip of the iceberg. A detailed look at the components within each silo begins to reveal the complexity brought about by the redundancy and duplication in today's IT infrastructure.

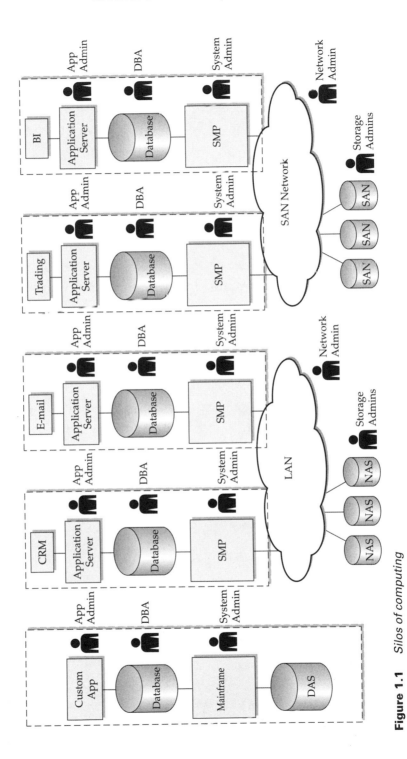

Figure 1.1   *Silos of computing*

Hardware Infrastructure

Hardware infrastructure comprises the physical components in the data centers such as storage, servers, and network switches. Enterprises currently have large numbers of isolated and heterogeneous hardware components. We'll examine two major components—storage and servers, in the following sections.

Storage

Enterprises have multiple storage islands—islands of direct-attached storage, islands of network-attached storage (NAS), and islands of storage-area networks (SAN). Often, these storage islands may have been formed over a period of time as storage is acquired from multiple vendors, by multiple business units, to satisfy diverse requirements for performance, high availability, security, and management. Even though the premise of NAS and SAN is to consolidate storage, limited interoperability among the offerings of the storage vendors has resulted in islands of NAS and islands of SAN storage.

Because the applications across these islands of storage have varying storage demands but do not share the storage resources, there is overall underutilization of storage. For example, there may be plenty of free space available in a storage array used for the data warehouse; however, it cannot be easily reassigned to the e-mail server. So, the IT department has to invest in purchasing a new file server to satisfy the needs of the e-mail system. This underutilization of storage results in high costs of storage for the enterprises.

Servers

Enterprises have servers from multiple vendors ranging from low-cost Intel/AMD–based servers to high-cost symmetric-multiprocessor systems (SMP) and mainframes. Traditionally, enterprises have deployed large SMP systems for each critical application, with an additional SMP of the same capacity as a standby for high availability and disaster recovery. Smaller, noncritical applications may share the SMP systems. However, the computing capacity of SMP systems (or mainframes) cannot be shared across the applications; hence, islands of server resources are formed.

Server resources are typically overprovisioned to the applications. Capacity is determined and allocated based on the estimated peak load and, in the case of critical applications, additional headroom capacity may be allocated to handle unexpected surges in demands. As each application has its own load characteristics, it is very unlikely that the peak-provisioned capacity of each application is used up at the same time. Thus, overall servers end up highly underutilized. Various surveys have put typical utilization of server resources to less than 30 percent.

Software Infrastructure

Software infrastructure includes software used to develop, deploy, and run enterprise applications such as operating systems, databases, application platform suites, and application development environments.

Operating Systems

IT departments usually manage a heterogeneous array of operating system environments. There may be several flavors of Unix systems, Linux systems, Windows systems, and so on. Even on the same flavor of Unix, different servers may be on different versions or may have different patches. Because each of these systems has to be managed individually, it results in high-cost of management for the systems and the applications running on them. For example, an application running on one system is expected to run well on another one with similar configuration. But differences in the patch levels on two systems may cause the application to fail. Such a difference in behavior is very difficult and costly to diagnose.

Databases

Enterprises may have deployed one database for each application. Same applications used within different business units may store data in separate databases. Each such database is designed, configured, and tuned individually for the needs of that specific application. For critical applications, the database is configured on its own set of hardware. In case of noncritical applications, multiple databases may be run on the same hardware. This forms islands of databases and, more importantly, islands of information stored in these databases. While this approach addresses the needs of a particular application, it results in several problems, discussed in the sections that follow.

Underutilization of Database Resources Since each application has its own database, these applications do not share available database capacity across them and the result is underutilization of database storage and processing resources. For example, an OLTP application is very active during the day, while a batch application is more active during the night. If these applications were both deployed on the same database, they could share the available database (and hence the underlying server and storage) capacity. But since they are deployed on different databases, they cannot share the available capacity.

High Cost of Database Management Database management has traditionally been a very time-consuming job, relying largely on the skill and experience of the individual DBA. Managing a database is a complex process from its initial deployment to regular maintenance such as taking backups, monitoring and tuning for performance and space allocation, performing regular upgrades, and applying patches. As each of these databases has to be managed individually by dedicated and highly skilled administrators, the result is high cost of database management.

High Cost of Information Management Islands of databases also cause information to be fragmented across many databases. It is easiest to provision information when it is consolidated in a single database. Fragmentation of information requires investing in and building information sharing solutions to address information availability needs of the enterprise.

Limited Scalability and Flexibility A standalone database when deployed on an SMP has limited scalability and can address the application growth to the limited degree (i.e., size of the SMP). When the application scalability needs reach beyond this limit, a larger and usually more expensive SMP server must be purchased.

Application Platform Suites

With the advent of the Internet, most business applications these days run in a multitier architecture, one of the tiers being an application server. An application server typically comprises a web cache, a web server, and a Java layer. Application server offerings may also include Java development tools, business integration offerings, portals, and so on, collectively referred to as application platform suites (APS). A typical large enterprise uses application servers and platform suites from multiple vendors. Even though it is possible to run multiple applications on the same application server, typically enterprises deploy each application on its own separate application server. By now, you may see that such a solution suffers from the similar problems as outlined in the databases section—underutilization of application server resources, high management costs for these application servers, and lack of scalability and flexibility to address the growth in application needs.

Business Application and Process Infrastructure

Running on top of the hardware and software infrastructure is the application layer, which encapsulates the actual business logic. It consists of business applications, business processes, and workflows.

Business Applications

Enterprises build and acquire many applications over the course of time. Some of these are packaged applications that have been customized to suit their needs. Such packaged applications include CRM and ERP applications from Oracle, SAP, and others, as well as complex industry-specific applications. Enterprises also have home-grown or custom-built applications that may have evolved over a number of years. These applications may be written in a variety of programming paradigms such as Java, .NET, XML, C, etc. They have a variety of online-transaction processing (OLTP) applications and decision support system (DSS) applications.

Each business unit may deploy applications independently at different times. Depending on the IT decisions made at the time of deployment, the application may be run on different underlying hardware, operating systems, databases, storage, etc. For example, the order-processing system may be deployed on a Linux-based platform and the e-mail system on a

Windows server. Sometimes the same software and hardware are deployed and configured differently by each business unit. The end result is that IT departments have to manage a complex heterogeneous mix of hardware platforms, software, vendor packages, and custom-built applications.

Business Workflows

Enterprise applications need to collaborate with each other to perform a business function. For example, an order-entry application takes the order from customers, the billing application bills the customer, the order-processing application processes the order, and the shipping application ships the orders. Packaged applications from a single vendor today are largely single monolithic pieces of software that are highly integrated to perform a specific business function, typically specific to an industry. At the time of initial deployment, these applications are configured and customized to match the enterprise business model. Unfortunately, this means that the business workflows within the applications are largely hardwired and cannot be changed easily. When using applications from different vendors or with legacy systems, applications have to be integrated to create a business workflow using some manner of integration technology. A number of enterprise integration vendors provide integration products such as integration hubs, brokers, etc., based on their own proprietary protocols. As a result, enterprise application integration typically involves extensive customization via large and expensive software development projects. None of these approaches allow the efficiency and agility in business processes that enterprises would like to have today.

Operational Elements

Enterprise IT departments must follow various operational processes in order to ensure smooth running of the infrastructure and business application layers. These operational aspects include maintaining separate development, testing, production and systems, as well as monitoring and managing performance, security, and availability of the IT infrastructure.

Development, Testing, and Production Systems

Large enterprises have separate development, testing, and production systems. The staff responsible for all these systems is different. These include various sets of storage administrators, system administrators, DBAs, and application developers.

The process to move an application from a development environment to a testing environment, and then from testing to production systems is largely manual and therefore error prone. Typically, each business unit goes through its own set of testing before deploying any new software. As a result, enterprises end up with different IT systems running diverse software releases and on different patch set levels.

Performance

Different business applications require differing levels of performance guarantees. For instance, with an online store, it is not acceptable to make a customer wait for over a few seconds to take an order. However, in a reporting system it may be alright if the query does not return the data for a few minutes. Further, the load on various systems may change over the course of the month or year. The problem is that when infrastructure for each application is provisioned independently, it must account for the peak expected load of each application. As a result some systems may remain idle for large periods of time and unexpected surges cannot be handled effectively. Ideally, systems must be able to scale up to sporadic increases in load without remaining underutilized during normal operation. This is not easy to achieve when the idle computing power is locked up in a silo in a different data center.

Security

In IT environments today, each IT system is configured for its own specific security requirements. Each server, database, and application server is managed individually for security. Diverse configurations of software coupled with perpetual threats of intrusion and viruses make managing enterprise systems security a very daunting task.

Another aspect of security is the management of user identities for use with various applications. User accounts are typically provisioned or deprovisioned separately for each application individually. Any error in doing so may result in an extremely costly security breach.

Finally, regulatory requirements such as Sarbanes-Oxley and HIPAA are also pushing for stricter security controls on enterprise data to prevent accidental or intentional tampering. This has put increasing pressure on enterprise security management.

High Availability

IT environments require a "downtime" window to perform maintenance activities. However, with the growing trend of global business operations, enterprises need 24×7 availability or very limited downtimes for their critical systems.

Different business units deploy different solutions and architectures for high availability. Almost every critical application has its own equally powerful redundant hardware as a spare in case of system failure. Events like September 11 have further highlighted the importance of having a disaster recovery strategy for business continuity. This means that huge amounts of hardware must be kept deployed, perhaps idle, at an alternate location, which is a huge cost to the enterprise.

Summary

Enterprises today need to be agile and efficient in order to meet competitive and economic pressures. To achieve this goal, enterprises require an IT infrastructure that is flexible to meet changing computational and operational business needs and also cost-effective to make efficient use of existing assets. IT architecture is inherently complex due to the many components and operational aspects involved. Islands of infrastructure exacerbate this complexity and in addition, result in tremendous underutilization of IT systems, putting a huge cost burden on the enterprise.

The next chapter will describe how the Enterprise Grid Computing model presents a novel approach to solve these problems and how it can be applied to Oracle environments.

2

Introduction to Enterprise Grid Computing

In Chapter 1, we discussed the demands of business and the complex issues faced with the current enterprise IT architecture. Enterprise grid computing provides a model to evolve enterprise architecture incrementally to meet these business demands. Enterprise grid computing rationalizes the islands of IT infrastructure within an enterprise and consolidates them into one global infrastructure, an enterprise grid. Concepts of enterprise grid computing can be applied independently and incrementally to the various layers of the IT such as servers, storage, databases, application servers, applications, information, etc., based on the compelling business needs.

In this chapter, we provide an overview of the changes brought about by the enterprise grid computing model, via technology, people, and processes, at each layer of the IT stack. We discuss the benefits of the enterprise grid computing model and what it means to different people in an organization. We also mention relevant technologies that specifically benefit enterprises using Oracle. Chapter 5 will focus on how to incrementally evolve an existing IT architecture towards the enterprise grid computing model.

Enterprise Grid Computing Defined

At the highest level, the central idea of grid computing is computing as a utility. The user of the grid should not care where the data resides or which computer processes the requests. Instead, the user should be able to

13

request information or computations and have them delivered according to his or her needs and in a timely fashion. This is analogous to the way electric utilities work, in that you do not know where the generator is or how the electric grid is wired, you just ask for electricity, and you get it. The goal is to make computing a utility, a commodity, and ubiquitous, hence the name—*The Grid* [Oracle Grid 2002].

From the perspective of a provider of the grid within an enterprise, grid computing is about providing an IT infrastructure that addresses the demands of business while utilizing the IT resources most efficiently and cost-effectively. We use the term *enterprise grid computing* to refer to grid computing within the bounds of a single enterprise. Enterprise grid computing is about ensuring that the resources such as computing power, storage, database, information, application services, etc., are allocated and available where and when there are needed. An IT infrastructure that provides enterprise grid computing can be referred to as an *enterprise grid*.

The Enterprise Grid Computing Model

The Enterprise Grid Computing model provides a rationalized architecture for enterprise IT. Figure 2-1 shows this architecture. At a high level, an enterprise architecture that follows an Enterprise Grid Computing model incorporates three essential characteristics—virtualization of resources, dynamic provisioning of resources to consumers, and centralized management of resources. Let us take a closer look at what each of these terms mean.

Virtualization Virtualization decouples the ownership of a resource from its consumer. Virtualization provides a layer between the resource and the consumer of the resource so that underlying resource can be replaced with a comparable resource without affecting the consumer. In an enterprise IT setting, consolidating all similar IT resources into a global pool is the first step towards virtualization. We use the term *resource* to mean both physical resources like servers, storage, and databases, as well as abstract resources like information and application logic.

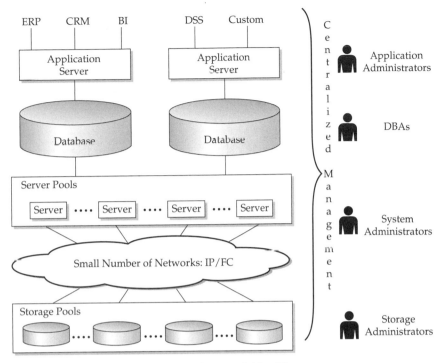

Figure 2.1   *Enterprise Grid Computing model for IT*

We will discuss specific aspects of virtualization for each layer of IT in the next section of this chapter.

Dynamic Provisioning Provisioning is the allocation of the resources to the consumers. In typical enterprise architectures today, provisioning of physical resources is statically done based on the expected peak demand of an application. However, in an enterprise where resources are virtualized and decoupled from a specific owner, they can be dynamically provisioned when required. Similarly, a resource can be deprovisioned when the application no longer requires it. Dynamic provisioning can also be applied to information. Once the source of information is virtualized, consumers do not need to know which system holds this information; it is simply delivered upon request.

Provisioning of resources in today's enterprises usually involves people who respond to the provisioning request and perform several manual steps to assign a resource. In the Enterprise Grid model, enterprises, over time, would move towards automated provisioning (using software) based on policies set up by a human being. Again, virtualization of resources and the ability to dynamically provision them make such automation possible. In the section that follows, we mention specific examples of automatic provisioning technologies available today.

Centralized Management   Though not inherent in the grid computing model, we consider centralized management of IT resources an essential element of enterprise grid computing. Centralized management provides control over all resources within the enterprise grid. Administrators can use centralized management to manage, monitor, and provision resources like servers, storage, databases, etc. In fact, dynamic provisioning of resources can be greatly simplified when similar resources are managed from a single viewpoint and use a common interface.

Enterprise Grid Computing at Different Layers of IT

In the following sections, we'll take a look at how, using technologies and processes, the three characteristics of virtualization, dynamic provisioning, and centralized management can be applied to different layers of IT. These characteristics can be applied to each layer of IT independently to gain grid computing benefits for that layer. We will mention technologies and products that apply specifically to Oracle environments.

Storage

Enterprise grid computing at the storage layer rationalizes the storage architecture by pooling together similar storage devices. Storage virtualization technologies assist in pooling the storage appliances from multiple vendors and storage appliances on traditionally separate SAN (FibreChannel) and NAS (IP) networks. Storage is provisioned to the applications based on the current needs of the application. When an application needs more storage, it is provided from the storage pool. Storage is allocated for the various applications based on the needs of business. For instance, high performance storage is allocated to mission-critical OLTP applications.

Various technologies from storage vendors assist in performing this storage virtualization and provisioning. A detailed discussion of these technologies is beyond the scope of this book. Oracle Automatic Storage Management (ASM) is a virtualization and provisioning technology included as part of Oracle Database 10g. Administrators simply provide disks to ASM, which in turn takes care of managing the storage allocation for the Oracle databases.

Servers

Enterprise grid computing at the server layer involves consolidating similar server resources into common pools. Server blades, which are standardized modular servers, can be used as building blocks to create a large pool of server resources. Multiple applications share the resources from these common pools. The resource allocations to those applications are changed dynamically based on the application workload or business needs.

A key technology for Oracle environments is Oracle Real Application Clusters (RAC), which virtualizes the server resources for the Oracle database by enabling a single database to be run on a group of servers. Similarly, Oracle Application Server can also run on a group of servers. Both RAC and Oracle Application Server provide the ability to dynamically add or remove server resources allocated to them.

In addition, Oracle offers technologies such as Oracle Streams and Oracle Transportable Tablespaces through which enterprises can easily offload certain processing (batch jobs, etc.) to a more available database and thus share server resources.

Databases

Enterprise grid computing at the database tier is about consolidating databases so that in place of creating a separate database for each application, a single database is used for multiple applications. It also involves virtualization of the database resource. For example, Oracle Database 10g includes the concept of a database service, which virtualizes the physical Oracle database instance to which an application connects.

A database can be composed of multiple database instances running on multiple servers and each of those instances can serve one or more of these applications via different services names. A connection just uses the service name without regard to the actual database instance or machine being used to serve the request.

In addition to virtualization, the service name allows the Oracle database to track and allocate resources to these various applications. For example, the payroll service may be allocated more resources than the human resources service, at month end, even though both may be served by the same underlying database.

Application Servers

Enterprise grid computing at the application server layer involves running multiple applications on a common set of application servers. Underlying server (CPU) resources can be allocated to the applications based on the application workload or business needs.

Oracle Application Server 10*g* has the capability of running multiple applications on one application server, using a cluster of servers. The Distributed Monitoring Service (DMS) of Oracle Application Server monitors a variety of resource utilization and the response time metrics for the various application server components and the applications. This information can be used to track the quality of service delivered by an application. Additionally, the system can be configured to raise an alert based on collected metrics, and to dynamically change resource allocations to meet the quality of service goals.

Applications

At the applications layer, enterprise grid computing is about moving to a service-oriented architecture (SOA). With SOA, enterprise applications and application modules, both homegrown and packaged, are exposed as services, typically Web Services. These services virtualize the encoded business logic and process flow, breaking the hard tie to an individual application, user interface, operating system, and programming language. This mechanism of exposing application logic as a service provides better software reuse as the same module can now be easily reused by many application developers. In addition, it also allows dynamic binding of these services, creating dynamic workflows. This ability to define and modify the workflows easily, allows enterprises to eke out efficiencies and improve their business processes. Thus, SOA enables a more agile and nimble application infrastructure to address new business requirements and competitive pressures.

The Oracle Application Server 10g suite offers comprehensive functionality to develop, deploy, manage, and orchestrate services. For example, the BPEL Process Manager allows business flows to be defined using the Business Process Execution Language (BPEL) and deployed using a graphical interface.

Information

Enterprise grid computing for information involves consolidating information (either physically or virtually) and making it available where it is needed.

The Oracle Database offers a number of information provisioning technologies to provision information depending on the needs of the enterprise. For example, if large amounts of information need to be shared, Oracle Transportable Tablespaces and Data Pump can be used to efficiently transfer data between databases. If information needs to be shared incrementally, Oracle Streams can be used to trickle feed data from one system to another. If data is accessed infrequently, it can be left in place and accessed on demand using distributed SQL technology.

Information originating at the business applications can be pooled together using data hubs, which serve as a single source for business-critical information. Data hubs use a variety of data integration technologies to pool together information sitting in multiple enterprise systems to create an accurate single source of truth. Instead of having to access several different systems to get information, business users access just the data hub. Oracle provides a number of Oracle Data Hubs that synchronize information in a single central location, from all systems throughout the enterprise. For example, the customer data hub provides an accurate, consistent, 360-degree view of enterprise's customer data, whether from packaged, legacy, or custom applications.

Centralized Management Technology

Centralized management is an essential element of enterprise grid computing. Consolidating and pooling similar resources make each layer of IT amenable to centralized management by itself. Many products exist that handle specific management functions for a given type of resource, like storage management software or blade provisioning software. However, even larger benefits can be obtained by managing the entire enterprise grid via a single interface.

Oracle Enterprise Manager with its Oracle Grid Control management console provides such a centralized management interface for the Oracle ecosystem. Oracle Grid Control supports the entire lifecycle management of IT infrastructure related to Oracle, including the database, application servers, OS, and other software. Grid Control handles the entire lifecycle from initial deployment to ongoing management, and eventually to decommissioning of a resource.

Grid Control provides a central console for the various administrators to manage and monitor specific resources they are responsible for. The home page for an administrator provides the overview of all managed resources.

Grid Control can also allow IT executives to gain more insight into IT operations by providing real-time information about the overall health of their IT infrastructure. They can monitor the quality of service delivered on critical business applications and obtain reports on the health and utilization of various IT resources.

Taking Strategic Steps Towards an Enterprise Grid

The discussion of enterprise grid computing thus far has focused on advances in technology, but grid computing requires more than just new technology. A successful grid strategy involves many significant changes to conventional IT processes. So how and where can an enterprise start this migration to The Grid? We believe that enterprises can incrementally evolve their current infrastructure towards enterprise grid computing by following three strategic steps: a) standardize components across the enterprise, b) consolidate IT infrastructure, and c) centralize and automate IT management functions. All three steps apply to both technology as well as IT processes.

Standardization helps in virtualization and pooling of resources. When the pool of resources consists of "similar" items, they can be replaced and re-allocated dynamically without impacting the consumer of the resource. To this end, enterprises could standardize server hardware, for example, using low-cost modular blades when replacing old hardware. Similarly, enterprises could standardize software products and software deployment configurations across multiple departments within the enterprise. Standardization could be achieved incrementally, for instance, when it is time to upgrade to a new version of the software. Consolidation involves sharing a single IT component among multiple consumers. As an example, enterprises could share a single Oracle database for multiple applications. Automation involves reducing human involvement in repetitive management tasks and procedures. For example, provisioning spare servers to meet a surge in demand or allocating storage to a database may be set up to be done with little assistance from the system administrator. We discuss these steps in greater detail in Chapter 5, "Steps to Grid Adoption."

Benefits of Enterprise Grid Computing

The Enterprise Grid Computing model provides several tangible benefits to enterprise IT.

Lower Costs of IT

Low-cost modular servers provide significant cost-savings on server investments. These are much cheaper than their SMP equivalents and offer savings in hardware acquisition costs, support costs, and management costs. It is also easier to pool and provision these modular servers. Hence, standardization on these servers can reduce the overall operational costs of the server infrastructure.

By pooling and dynamic-provisioning resources, enterprises can significantly reduce the overall cost of IT. Figure 2-2 illustrates the benefits of the enterprise grid computing model. Typically, OLTP applications are more active during the day while batch applications are more active during the night. Similarly, users in different parts of the world may be active at different times. In current IT environments, these applications have their own dedicated resources and hence an enterprise effectively ends up purchasing resources to handle the sum of peak load of all the applications. In the Enterprise Grid Computing model, applications share their resources. As all applications do not peak at the same time, the enterprise must now only acquire resources for the cumulative peak load of the applications. This results in substantial savings in the overall IT infrastructure costs. In addition, instead of allowing for headroom at each application for unexpected surges in demand, the headroom is shared by all these applications. This allows for more headroom capacity for all applications at a much lower cost.

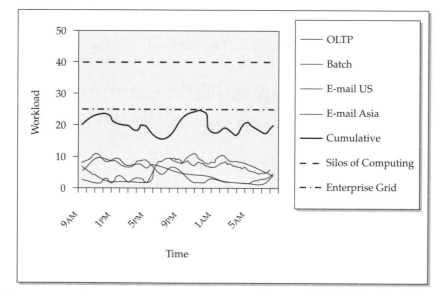

Figure 2.2   *Benefits of application resource sharing*

Consolidation also reduces the IT management costs by lowering the total number of components managed individually. Enterprises can manage multiple consolidated systems as a group and deploy the same set of management procedures to manage these systems. Further, enterprises can automate complex IT tasks. With consolidation and automation, administrators can really scale to manage more IT systems, thereby reducing IT management costs significantly.

Flexibility at Every Layer of the IT Stack

With the grid model, enterprises dynamically provision the required amount of resources to the applications from a pool of virtualized resources. Should an application need more resources to meet its service-level objectives, it is provided more resources. Should the resources no longer be required, the resources are taken away to be deployed elsewhere. This flexibility enables applications to continually meet their service-level objectives and deliver expected response times to business users and consumers. Applications can now also respond to the changing workload much faster.

Enterprise grid computing significantly reduces the time taken to deploy new systems or change business processes. Capacity needed to deploy the new systems is more readily available. By establishing automated system provisioning processes, enterprises are no longer hampered by long lead times to acquire new systems. Software provisioning technologies makes it easy to clone existing software configurations for deploying them on new systems—again reducing the deployment time significantly. SOA makes it easier to change the business processes flow and thus respond to changing business needs much faster.

Predictable Quality of Service

Oracle Grid Control (part of Oracle 10g) provides IT departments with tools and mechanisms to measure the quality of service delivered to their end users. CIOs can get better visibility into their IT systems. They can instantly know the response time that users in different parts of the world are experiencing and the throughput provided by various business applications. It is possible to know and keep track of which systems are up, which ones are down, and how long and how often they had unexpected outages.

Once the service levels being delivered to end users are measured and quantified, it becomes possible to change the resource allocations dynamically to be continually able to meet those service levels. Should there be a problem, it is much easier to identify and diagnose the root cause of the problem and fix it.

With enterprise grid computing, multiple applications can share redundant components that have been allocated for high availability purposes. As a result, not only is there better resource utilization, but also these applications now have access to more resources for fail-over or disaster recovery. This results in better availability for these applications and hence improves service to the end user.

Security of critical systems and applications is a key aspect of the overall quality of service of IT. As enterprises standardize their system configurations, best practice security policies can be deployed throughout the IT infrastructure. Oracle Grid Control helps in ensuring that enterprise-standardized best practices are followed and violations are fixed promptly. User provisioning in an enterprise grid can also be centralized at a single place. Instead of setting up users for each individual system, the user identity is set up just once and given access to specific systems via a mechanism such as single sign-on. This not only reduces the cost of security management but also makes IT more secure.

Why Enterprise Grid Computing with Oracle?

Enterprises can begin to benefit immediately from grid computing with even a modest initial investment, then as grid adoption grows within IT, so do the returns. The Oracle 10g platform includes numerous grid computing technologies today. Enterprises can start to use the grid model for Oracle environments and incrementally adopt newer grid technologies as they are developed in the future.

Support for Real Enterprise Applications

Oracle has grid-enabled the Oracle Database and the Oracle Application Server, and as a result, any application that runs on top of the Oracle platform is capable of benefiting from the grid model. No application rewrites are required to take advantage of the grid technologies such as Real Application Clusters (RAC), database virtualization using service names, and application server clustering for high availability. Other grid computing approaches may require a rewrite of the applications to leverage grid benefits. Providing those grid benefits inherently in the platform obviates the need for application rewrite.

Incremental Grid Adoption

Enterprises do not need to make a big leap into the world of enterprise grid computing. Oracle 10g offers numerous grid computing features at every layer of IT that can be adopted incrementally based on the current business needs. Enterprises can start with the grid technology that addresses their most critical business requirements and then incrementally adopt other grid features. For example, enterprises focusing on optimizing IT management can start with Oracle Grid Control, whereas enterprises focusing on server consolidation can start with Oracle's RAC technology.

Aligned for the Future

Grid technologies are evolving rapidly. The Oracle architecture and product directions are aligned to deliver future grid computing technologies. Oracle Database 10g is the first database designed for the grid. Enterprises' investments in Oracle are well leveraged as they can incrementally adopt additional grid computing technology as Oracle enhances its technology stack.

Throughout the Oracle 10g product stack, Oracle has implemented open standards wherever those standards are defined. Oracle is working with the Global Grid Forum and Enterprise Grid Alliance to help define grid standards. Oracle has supported and helped develop many standards such as ANSI, W3C, OASIS, and the Java Community Process. We can expect Oracle to continually support grid standards in its products as these standards evolve.

What Does Enterprise Grid Computing Mean to You?

Enterprise grid computing has something to offer to everyone across the enterprise.

CEOs

CEOs can implement new initiatives for business growth faster via the flexible IT infrastructure and business process architecture enabled by enterprise grid computing. At the infrastructure level, it allows faster provisioning of IT resources for a new business initiative. Existing IT infrastructure can be flexibly reallocated or a new one can be set up, without incurring long lead times.

At the applications layer, enterprise grid computing using SOA provides flexible business process architecture. In place of hardwired connections among enterprise applications, service-oriented architecture (SOA) makes it very flexible to deploy, manage, and orchestrate enterprise applications and business flows. The message flows among these various business processes can also be monitored. Monitoring reports of the critical business processes can provide CEOs with knowledge on how their businesses are operating, which can be utilized to identify new ways to optimize business.

Lines of Business

Some lines of business owners can be reluctant to move to pools of shared resources because they fear losing control and worry about not having access to the resources they need. In fact, when compared to typical enterprise architectures today, resources in a grid environment can be reallocated more dynamically so that the appropriate response time and throughput is continually delivered to their business applications, thereby better serving the lines of business. When lines of business need additional resources for new applications, resources in a grid can be reconfigured and deployed much faster than decentralized resources. Lines of business pay only for what they use and share the costs with other lines of business.

Some also fear that grid computing will reduce security of IT systems, but in practice the standardization, consolidation, and automation steps to grid computing actually enhance security. Enterprise-wide standardized security best practices can now be easily deployed across all IT systems. This improves the overall security by removing weak security links. Users are provisioned and deprovisioned at a central place rather than being set up at each application, again ensuring that lingering user accounts on satellite systems cannot lead to unauthorized access to critical systems. Single sign-on reduces the number of passwords that the users have to remember, which enables users to keep passwords truly secret, as they should be.

IT Executives

IT executives who are working with a constrained IT budget see lower costs and better returns on IT assets because of the increased utilization of their current IT resources. Enterprise grid computing lowers the costs of IT infrastructure, IT system management, and information management. Use of lower-cost industry standard hardware reduces the IT hardware costs. Use of industry-standard APIs and service-oriented architecture reduces the costs of software development and integration.

Grid computing technologies make it easier to automate operations on standardized and consolidated systems. This reduces overall system management costs. Oracle grid computing technologies provide IT executives with centralized management tools to monitor their IT systems, giving them better visibility into their IT systems. When they are asked about the status of IT, they do not need to call all their IT staff. They have information readily available. Highly available systems and better quality of service translate to happier lines of business, which also means better life for IT executives.

In place of making huge upfront investments in the IT infrastructure, CIOs can increase the capacity and pay as the business grows. Enterprises can deploy IT resources—hardware and software licenses—based on their current needs. As their needs increase, they acquire more hardware—storage and servers—dynamically, while keeping their systems online. Adding supplementary resources at various layers of IT does not increase management tasks. Hence, IT executives can scale their IT staff to manage more IT systems.

IT Staff

Today, the life of IT staff is frequently reduced to managing fire drills. With enterprise grid computing, IT staff can become more proactive. IT staff is notified of the problem even before it arises so that it can be addressed before there is a fire drill. Many IT problems, when managed reactively, can cause a ripple effect throughout the IT infrastructure. Proactive IT management reduces the repercussions of any individual unpredicted problem. As a result, IT staff can now have more time to plan other strategic tasks.

With Oracle grid computing technologies, daily mundane performance tuning and performance diagnostic tasks are reduced. Oracle databases and application servers are increasingly becoming more self-managing. These systems check for problems within themselves and try to fix them by themselves. For things that administrators care about, alerts can be raised. Instead of constantly monitoring the systems themselves, administrators can simply set up policies for what the system should notify them about. Once alerted, they can often address the problem even before it becomes severe and causes IT dysfunctions.

IT staff also have information about their systems at hand all the time. They can monitor their systems using a single graphical tool, Oracle Grid Control. They do not need to look at every system individually to find the status of those systems.

Summary

Enterprise grid computing is a powerful concept that provides solutions to a number of problems faced by enterprises today. Specifically, this model brings together the currently fragmented enterprise resources into a common pool, from which resources are assigned and reallocated to consumers as need arises. All resources are managed centrally using a common interface. There is a move towards automation at every layer of the IT stack, including storage, servers, databases, and application servers. Enterprise grid computing offers flexibility at the application and business process layers by using service-oriented application architectures. Enterprises based on the Oracle environment can embark on the path to grid computing using already available technologies from Oracle and other industry vendors.

In the next chapter, we will take a broader look at grid computing. We will provide a brief history of enterprise grid computing and its ongoing evolution from use in scientific and technical computing to the current state of the art. We will also mention the standards activities and the relevant players in this domain and the general direction in which the industry is headed. Different vendors call it by different names and there is a lot of industry-specific terminology floating around, but enterprise grid computing is a powerful concept, and it is here to stay.

References

[Oracle Grid 2002] Goyal, B. and Souder, B. Oracle and the Grid (an Oracle White paper). Nov 2002. http://www.oracle.com/technology/products/oracle9i/grid_computing/OracleGridWP.pdf

3

The Evolution of Grid Computing

A search on Google or Yahoo will find many different definitions of grid computing and a number of ways to classify it. Grid computing is a vast problem space. Different organizations across both research and industry are actively working on different aspects of the problem, leading to different definitions and viewpoints. This chapter classifies grid computing along the lines of its evolution from its origins to its present form, specifically from the point of view of enterprise computing. First, we will look at several proposed definitions of grid computing and the terms that industry vendors have used to refer to grid. Next, we will mention concepts and terms commonly used in context of grid computing. Finally, we will cover industry trends that have put enterprises on the path towards grid computing.

Grid Classification and Evolution

Like the Internet, the concept of grid computing started in scientific and research organizations in an attempt to share resources across universities. It was applied to scientific and technical problems. It found an early use in enterprises for solving computationally intensive problems such as financial modeling. The same concept of sharing resources was later adapted to enterprise applications and IT infrastructure resulting in the paradigm known as enterprise grid computing.

We believe that next in line, after enterprise grids within a single enterprise, will be grids across enterprises or across partner organizations. This would likely be followed by the realization of the grand vision of grid, which is "computing as a utility." This is when we would see the emergence of computing utility providers similar to power grid providers. Over time, enterprises will move away from hosting and managing their own IT and will instead use the services of computing utility providers.

We discuss each of these stages in the evolution of grid computing in the following sections. In the course of reading these sections, you may notice that boundaries in terms of both timeline and use cases among these various stages are somewhat fuzzy. For example, the work to fully address the needs of both the scientific and technical computing as well as enterprise computing is happening in parallel. In addition, there already exist the early examples of grids across partner organization and computing as a utility.

Grid for Scientific and Technical Computing

Grid computing has its origins at universities and research labs where it was used to solve high performance computing and batch processing problems. Scientists and researchers used grid computing to collaborate with scientists at other universities and to share their computational resources.

SETI@home is one of the early and popular applications of grid computing in this space. SETI (Search for Extraterrestrial Intelligence) project analyzed radio frequency data from signals gathered by radio telescopes to identify patterns indicating intelligent life. This is a very computing-intensive application and hence no single research lab could provide the computing power needed for it. The scientists came up with an ingenious solution. With household PCs and desktop systems becoming quite powerful and Internet connectivity becoming ubiquitous, idle cycles on these machines could be used to help with the number-crunching needs of the SETI analysis. Users download a small program on their desktop. When the desktop is idle, the downloaded program would detect it and use the idle machine cycles. When connected back to the Internet, it would send the results back to the central site. The net computing power of idle PCs across the world could be significant enough to perform complex numerical analysis.

CERN, a pioneering research organization involved in the development of the Web, is also among the early scientific and research users of the grid. CERN is building a Large Hadron Collider (LHC) Computing Grid to manage data generated by the LHC experiments. The largest experiments will generate over one petabyte of data per year. Around 2000 users and 150 institutes will be involved in conducting and analyzing the data from these experiments. Analyzing such large quantity of data requires computing resources well beyond the capability of a single institution. The LHC Computing Grid provides a coherent computing environment for collaboration across these institutes. It also allows researchers to utilize computational resources from the grid to tackle immense computational problems.

In 1996, scientists at Argonne National Lab and the University of Southern California started the Globus project to develop and share common tools and technologies for developing such grids. They also started the Grid Forum, North America. In March 2001, the Grid Forums around the world (the Grid Forum from North America, the Grid Forum from Asia Pacific, and the European Grid Forum) merged together to create the Global Grid Forum (GGF). Industry vendors have since joined the Global Grid Forum, and the work in the GGF now encompasses requirements from the commercial sector as well.

In 1998, the Globus project released the first version of the Globus Toolkit, v1.0, which has since undergone many revisions. The Globus Toolkit, released as open source software, is being used in a number of scientific and commercial high-performance computing applications. There are two organizations that have been started to commercialize the use of Globus Toolkit—the Globus Consortium and Univa. The Globus Consortium is a consortium of industry vendors whose goal is to provide direction for commercial use to the Globus Toolkit to better handle the requirements for enterprise computing. Univa is an independent company that supports and drives use of the Globus Toolkit in the enterprise world, similar to what RedHat did for Linux.

The problems solved by these early grids share a common thread. These applications are all either big-batch applications or high-performance technical applications that can be broken down into smaller pieces, and their computation can be spread across a large number of independent machines. These applications are rewritten to make use of grid computing. A majority of applications in the enterprises are packaged applications such as ERP, CRM, HR, etc., or home-grown applications that have been developed over a number of years in different programming paradigms such as C, Java, and .NET. Some of these applications use software from a number of software vendors. In general, these applications cannot be broken down into smaller pieces. Also, enterprises have invested a lot in these applications, making it extremely cost-prohibitive to rewrite them. Thus, the concept of grid computing could not work "as is" in an enterprise setting. This leads us to the next section on enterprise grid computing.

Enterprise Grid

Around 2000/2001, major industry vendors such as Oracle, IBM, HP, Intel, Sun, etc., realized the potential of the idea of resource sharing used in scientific grid computing and started to become actively involved in this space. These vendors wanted to adapt and use grid computing in the context of enterprise applications and IT infrastructure. It was apparent that enterprise applications were fundamentally different from scientific applications. The vendors instead began to focus on the problem of sharing infrastructure within an enterprise data center. This meant streamlining data center operations, increasing efficiency, and reducing overall IT costs. Thus, grid computing in the enterprise is about pooling data center resources and allocating these resources for the needs of multiple enterprise applications, and managing these data center resources more efficiently while delivering the required quality of service to business users. In this manner, the grid computing concept from the scientific world morphed into a powerful paradigm for enterprise resource sharing and efficiency.

At the time of this writing, nearly all major industry vendors have embraced the concept of enterprise grid computing. Different vendors use different terms such as adaptive enterprise (HP), autonomic computing (IBM), on-demand (numerous), utility computing (Veritas), and N1 (Sun), but these terms all refer to enterprise grid computing. With the growing awareness of grid computing, some vendors have even renamed their product family for grid computing. Notable among these are Oracle with its Oracle 10*g* product family and Network Appliance with its Data ONTAP™ 7G platform and V-Series (formerly called gFiler) product line.

As industry vendors started actively participating in the grid efforts at the Global Grid Forum, they realized that this was a very large problem space that would take many years to address fully. In the meantime, there was a need for an organization that would focus on the immediate needs of enterprises. In April 2004, a group of industry vendors founded the Enterprise Grid Alliance (EGA) with the goal to promote and enable grid computing within the boundaries of a single enterprise. Now, GGF, EGA, and other standard bodies such as W3C, OASIS, DMTF, SNIA, and IETF, all work together via liaison relationships to advance standards for grid computing.

Whenever embracing a paradigm shift, it is important, for business and economic reasons, to incrementally evolve rather than make a single giant leap. With regard to enterprise grid computing, enterprises would like to evolve their IT infrastructure, leveraging their past investments in storage, servers, databases, application servers, packaged applications, legacy applications, management tools, and other ISV software. The good news is that enterprises are able to lay a path forward towards grid computing by embarking on standardization, consolidation, and automation projects.

The latest advancements in technology offerings in the storage, servers, databases, application servers, and the management tools space are all in alignment with the concept of the enterprise grid. As an example, enterprise grid computing at the infrastructure layer (servers, storage, databases, and application servers) can be implemented on a platform like Oracle 10*g*. Oracle 10*g* platform provides numerous technologies for efficient utilization of IT infrastructure to meet the needs of enterprise applications without the need to rewrite them. These technologies can be adopted incrementally while leveraging existing IT investments, thus easing the grid adoption path for the enterprises. Chapter 5 will provide some detailed guidelines in this regard.

Enterprise grid computing at the applications layer is manifested with Service-Oriented Architecture (SOA). SOA enables loose coupling of applications from different vendors and platforms by exposing them as services. This allows pieces of application functionality to be reused and repurposed without writing an entire new application from scratch. This in effect breaks up monolithic application silos into a pool of reusable application components, from which larger applications such as business workflows can be dynamically constructed.

Emerging technology standards like Web Services and Business Process Execution Language (BPEL) are instrumental in such an application grid. There is a lot of work being done in standard bodies such as W3C and OASIS (discussed in Chapter 4) to provide standards for communication and information exchange across applications using Web Services. As these standards mature, one can foresee application grids spanning businesses or business partners. This leads us to our next stage in grid evolution, which is grid across partner organizations.

Grid Across Partner Organizations

The idea of grid across sister organizations is not entirely new. Early examples are found in the scientific and research community, where grid computing is used to share computing resources across collaborating universities. There are many examples of these grids including the United States National Science Foundation (NSF)–funded TeraGrid project and CERN's LHC Computing Grid (discussed earlier). TeraGrid is a multiyear effort to build and deploy the world's largest, fastest, distributed infrastructure for open scientific research. When completed, the TeraGrid will include 20 teraflops of computing power distributed at five sites, facilities capable of managing and storing nearly one petabyte of data, high-resolution visualization environments, and toolkits for grid computing.

In the enterprise world, the life sciences industry has the potential to offer the first examples of partner grids to share data across many companies. Drug discovery involves a very long cycle of collaboration over a number of years, spanning multiple organizations. These organizations have to share vast amounts of research data. There are also vast amounts of public and private bioinformatics data sitting in different data banks, such as NCBI, around the world. Drug discovery involves analyzing and preserving all the information for regulatory reasons.

There is a vast amount of information that needs to be shared in almost every industry. It is possible to create a number of industry-specific data hubs that provide a central place for sharing information across that industry. Oracle's CEO Larry Ellison talked about this concept at his keynote at the Oracle Openworld conference in December 2004. An example of such a data hub can be a global credit database, a database put together by all the world's credit agencies that would hold all their customers' credit records. When someone applies for credit, this global database is checked, and a decision is made based on its contents. This global database is in fact, however, a data hub, with individual institutions copying their credit records into the hub to provide a consolidated view of the credit market. There can be other data hubs, such as Financial Services Data Hub created by SEC, Life Sciences Data Hub created by FDA, and so on.

On the enterprise applications side, partner grids could involve business partners such as suppliers and consumers, seamlessly conducting their business over the Internet using Web Services. Business is conducted as if their IT infrastructures are intertwined, appearing as if they were a single IT infrastructure. Yet at the same time, these collaborations are flexible so that one partner can be readily replaced by another one and perhaps even automatically. In the boom days of the Internet, there were many companies doing Business-to-Business eCommerce, e.g., Commerce One. These companies were the early examples of partner grids on the enterprise applications side. B2B eCommerce today is conducted using home-grown or proprietary technologies. Advances in Web Services technology should help to standardize and simplify, and thus also advance B2B eCommerce and partner grids.

Computing as a Utility

"Computing as a utility" is the blue sky of enterprise grid computing. As data center infrastructure and management become increasingly standardized and automated, managed IT starts to become an attractive proposition. In place of owning and managing their own data centers, enterprises can just focus on their core competency and let someone else manage their IT operations. They pay based on the amount of resources such as servers, storage, databases, or application services they use.

Some large enterprises are already moving towards the "IT as a service" model. In these companies, IT is a profit-and-loss center that provides computing service to other business units. Business units have service level agreements (SLAs) for their business applications that IT has to meet. IT in return charges the business units based on the amount of computing power used.

There have been instances when large enterprises have sold their data centers to service providers such as EDS, TCS, IBM, or HP. Enterprises enter into annual or multiyear agreements with their service providers who are then responsible for delivering the required quality of service for enterprise applications in return for a subscription fee. The service providers can sell the computing power to the original enterprise and to other enterprises.

In December 2004, Sun Microsystems, Inc. launched the Grid Utility service that charges $1 per CPU per hour for processing resources and $1 per gigabyte per month for storage capacity. Sun claims that this service can be used for applications such as modeling, simulations, and movie rendering.

Application Service Providers (ASPs) are yet another example of computing utility providers. ASPs supply software applications and/or software-related services over the Internet. Corio (acquired by IBM), Oracle on Demand, Celoxis, etc., are all examples of ASPs. Enterprises access software applications hosted and managed by the ASP over the Internet and pay based on use. It will take time for computing to be as ubiquitous as electricity and to be produced and delivered as electricity. But we believe the early examples indicate that this is where computing is headed.

Grid Definitions and Related Terms

One of the reasons for the confusion surrounding grid computing is its usage in multiple domains—scientific, academic, and industry. Further, there has been a proliferation of vendor specific terms and slogans that all refer to the same concept. In the following sections, we will lay out some of the common definitions and terminology that are encountered in discussing grid computing. This will also help the reader to understand the industry-wide nature of interest in this concept, albeit under different names.

What Is Grid Computing?

A search on the Internet will find many distinct definitions of grid. In this section, we list some popular definitions of grid and provide context in which those definitions are proposed. We believe the only difference in these definitions is the emphasis on different aspects of the grid. The end goal of all these definitions is exactly the same.

- In 1998, Carl Kesselman and Ian Foster in the book *The Grid: Blueprint for a New Computing Infrastructure* provided the definition of grid computing as this: "A computational grid is a hardware and software infrastructure that provides dependable, consistent, pervasive, and inexpensive access to high-end computational capabilities." This definition was clearly inspired by the then prevailing use of grid computing in the scientific and research space, where grid computing was used to share high-end computational resources across universities.

- A few years later, Oracle began to get involved in this space. Leaders at Oracle—Benny Souder et al, (including one of the authors of this book)—were thinking of ways of applying grid computing to the enterprise space. They realized that eventually grids may be "geographically distributed," "heterogeneous," and "cross-organizational boundaries," but they must first be realized within the domain of a single organization, on a group of homogeneous resources, located at the same data center. This approach helps enterprises in realizing grid benefits today rather than many years hence. From this new viewpoint, enterprise grid computing is comprised of three elements: a) virtualization, b) provisioning, and c) scale out. Virtualization breaks the static link between resources allocated to the application. Provisioning allocates the resources to the applications dynamically. Scaling out provides the flexibility

to add more resources and to move more applications to this grid.
These three elements combine to provide the benefits of better resource utilization and flexible IT infrastructure to the enterprises.

- The Enterprise Grid Alliance (EGA) has provided a consensual
  definition among the industry vendors that focuses on the functionality a grid can provide to enterprise data centers. Rather
  than defining grid as specific components, attributes, or configurations—which change over time as technology changes—the Enterprise
  Grid Alliance (EGA) defines grid computing as a style of computing.
  According to EGA [EGA Roadmap], at the highest level, enterprise
  grid computing is characterized by an architecture that aggregates
  IT resources into dynamically assignable pools managed at a higher
  level of abstraction, enabling organizations to:

  - Provision resources to dynamically meet application requirements
    and business priorities;

  - Consolidate computing components into a few large resource
    pools, simplifying provisioning tasks;

  - Standardize computing components, configurations, processes,
    and applications across an enterprise; and

  - Scale as resources and workloads grow.

- While EGA has focused itself on the enterprise data centers, the
  Global Grid Forum (GGF) has taken a more expansive role and has
  defined grid as: "A system that is concerned with the integration,
  virtualization, and management of services and resources in a
  distributed, heterogeneous environment that supports collections
  of users and resources (virtual organizations) across traditional
  administrative and organizational domains (real organizations)."
  [GGF OGSA Glossary] GGF aims to enable grid computing in its
  most generic sense. Hence in this definition, the term *resource* encompasses not only entities that are pooled (e.g., hosts, software
  licenses, IP addresses) or that provide a given capacity (e.g., disks,
  networks, memory), but also processes, print jobs, and virtual
  organizations.

The scientific and research and GGF definitions are broader definitions that attempt to cover all possible use cases. This makes the problem very broad and requires solutions that take a long time to develop. Oracle and the other EGA vendors are focusing on a subset that's most essential for the enterprise grid use case in an effort to expeditiously provide solutions for what they believe to be the largest and most important class of users, the enterprises.

Industry Terms for Grid Computing

Industry vendors and analysts have used a variety of terms for grid computing, which unfortunately has also created a good deal of confusion in the minds of enterprise users. All these terms refer to the same underlying concept of grid computing. Some of the popular terms are listed here.

Autonomic Computing Vendors using the term *autonomic computing* include IBM, HP, and Intel. Autonomic computing is the vision that the computing systems would align themselves according to the defined priorities and goals by administrators, similar to the self-healing, self-management capability of human body that dynamically adjusts itself to its environment and protects itself from various challenges. The essence of autonomic computing is developing software and hardware components that are self-managing and self-healing in order to address the problem of managing complex data centers. The autonomic computing vision of dynamic alignment of data center resources to meet business objectives is exactly what grid computing promises to deliver.

Utility Computing Many vendors such as Veritas and Sun are using the term *utility computing* for grid computing. Utility computing encompasses two aspects. The first aspect is the view of computing as a utility, when delivery and consumption of computing parallels electricity. As a user of the grid, you do not care where your computing is done or where your information is, all you care about is to get your computation done and to get your information when you need it and where you need it. The second aspect is chargeback or the pay-per-use view of computing, where users of the computing infrastructure pay for the amount of the computing resource they consume.

On Demand Computing *On demand* is another term used for grid computing by numerous vendors. The on demand computing model is a concept in which computing resources are made available to the users as needed. The concept can also be applied to other aspects of IT infrastructure besides computing power. Aligning IT resources to the needs of business and providing information to the consumers, business executives, CIOs, and CEOs as needed, both fall under the on demand vision. The objectives of on demand computing and those of enterprise grid computing essentially coincide.

Real-Time Enterprise The term *real-time enterprise*, coined by Gartner, is used in the context of making application infrastructure more flexible via Web Services. However, in the broadest sense, the term real-time enterprise, like grid computing, applies to making IT and the information infrastructure flexible to meet the needs of the business. It also refers to enabling Service-Oriented Architecture for applications, which allows business processes and workflows to be morphed or adapted to exploit greater process efficiencies or new market requirements.

Service-Oriented Computing *Service-oriented computing* is often used interchangeably with Service-Oriented Architecture and Web-Services–based computing. In its most general sense, service-oriented computing is synonymous with grid computing. A service is the capability delivered by the data center components, including storage, server, and network at the physical layer; database and application server at the infrastructure layer; and applications and business flows at the business process platform layer. Service-oriented computing is about delivering these services with the desired quality of service along with cost-effective and agile IT for the enterprise.

Adaptive Computing or Adaptive Enterprise The terms *adaptive computing* and *adaptive enterprise*, more commonly used by HP, are used similarly to autonomic computing. With adaptive computing, the computing infrastructure aligns or reconfigures itself based on the changing workload and/or business needs.

Terminology Relevant to Grid Computing

Along with the definitions of grid computing itself, a number of terms have come into use regarding the capabilities or features of a grid computing solution. Here are some useful terms and concepts that are used in the context of grid computing.

Virtualization *Virtualization* breaks the static ties between IT component and its consumer. In the traditional IT environments, IT components are statically allocated to their consumers. In the grid computing environments, these allocations are dynamic. Virtualization adds a layer onto an IT component so that the new component exhibits the interface properties of the original. This layer hides the true implementation of the virtualized object so that the original can be replaced or changed without impacting the interaction of entities that have a dependency on it.

Provisioning *Provisioning* is the allocation of IT components for use by their consumers. In current IT environments, provisioning is static, i.e., once the IT components are allocated for a specific purpose, those allocations are not changed, whereas in the grid computing environments, provisioning is dynamic. The allocation of resources for various applications is changed over time based on load or business needs.

Service-Oriented Architecture *Service-Oriented Architecture* (SOA) is an architectural style whose goal is to achieve loose coupling among interacting services. Services provide object-oriented encapsulation for business logic or IT component functions. Typically, Web Services are used to perform interactions in the Service-Oriented Architecture. A number of standards organizations such as OASIS and W3C are working on the Web Services specifications for Service-Oriented Architecture.

Industry Trends

Industry trends are inadvertently taking the enterprises towards grid computing. In the following sections, we briefly review some of the key trends that have facilitated the movement toward enterprise grid computing.

Hardware Trends

Moore's Law has been applicable to almost every aspect of hardware. Performance of the hardware components has increased significantly and at the same time the costs have gone down significantly. The result is that very few enterprises now invest in custom hardware for performance reasons. The emphasis is now on ease of management and low cost. This has led to increased standardization of hardware within enterprises.

Storage Disks

Storage disks have become commoditized. People can buy so-called JBODs (Just a Bunch of Disks) and put them in RAID configuration. The value in the storage infrastructure has now moved up the chain. Storage vendors provide storage platforms for the enterprise data centers that are built using these commodity disks but are reliable, high-available, resilient, and easy and efficient to manage.

Low-Cost Modular Servers

On the server side, Intel has driven the mass production of CPUs. This has resulted in commoditization of servers. Enterprises are deploying en masse low-cost modular servers comprised of one to four CPUs. Most popular form factors for these modular servers are rack-optimized servers and blade servers. Each server in a rack-optimized configuration is a complete computer in itself. These servers are placed in a common rack. Blade frames (or racks) for the blade servers are more sophisticated as these blades share components such as power, cooling, etc. Blade frame also provides a sophisticated network fabric that provides efficient connectivity among these blades. The cost of a system built using several modular servers can be drastically lower than that of an equivalent SMP (symmetric multiprocessor) system.

High-Speed, Low-Latency Interconnects

Networking speed is continually increasing. 1Gb Ethernet is now a standard up from 10Mb. 10Gb Ethernet and Infiniband are also making inroads into enterprise data centers. Advances in the networking are increasing the throughput and decreasing the latency for network communications. These advances are in turn driving cluster computing and increasing the performance and encouraging the adoption of distributed computing.

Software Trends

Software trends also indicate that standardization is becoming very important at the infrastructure layer, such as operating systems software. Over the past few years, standards have been developed for much of the application development and business logic infrastructures, strongly favoring Service-Oriented Architectures.

Linux

Linux is the fastest growing operating system today and is now an accepted platform for enterprise computing. Growth in popularity of Linux is one of the drivers for standardization of OS platforms within enterprise environments. The many flavors of Unix are slowly dwindling, reducing the heterogeneity in enterprise environments.

Java and Web Services

Java is now the de facto platform for application development. JCP (Java Community Process) has provided a number of Java specifications (JSRs: Java Specification Requests) that have helped in modularizing and standardizing application development. JSRs provide standard building blocks for commonly used functions and are modularizing application development.

Web Services provide a standard mechanism to discover and invoke application modules. Growing adoption of Web Services and Web Services standards provide efficient and standard mechanisms for loose coupling of application modules and orchestration of the business processes using them.

Grid-Enabling Technologies

Almost every major industry vendor is talking about and working on the grid computing technologies. Vendors have different approaches to incorporate grid technologies in their software. Some vendors are offering technologies that enterprises can use to build grid-enabled applications. Oracle has a unique approach in that it is grid-enabling its own software so that at the infrastructure layer (servers and storage) the applications built on the Oracle platform are automatically grid-enabled.

Enterprise Trends

Economic and competitive pressures are forcing enterprises towards making more cost-effective and efficient use of their IT assets. These trends are also taking enterprises towards "IT as a service" model.

Consolidation

Enterprises have realized the inefficiencies of silo-ed environments. Driven by the motto of reducing cost and increasing efficiencies, enterprises are moving towards consolidation of their IT infrastructures. As enterprises move towards consolidation, grid computing provides them with the architectural and process model for efficiently aligning their IT resources to their application and business needs and to manage their IT efficiently.

IT as a Service

Certain enterprises are moving towards "IT as a service" model to make IT more accountable in delivering better quality of service to business users. They are transforming IT to a profit-and-loss center that provides computing service to the other business units. IT charges the other business units based on their consumption of the IT resources.

Regulatory Trends

Globally there are increased regulations, e.g., HIPAA and Sarbanes-Oxley, governing corporate operations and financial accounting. These regulations are driving enterprises to take a closer look and streamline their processes, reduce information fragmentation, and increase security. As enterprises undertake projects for regulatory compliance, they find themselves adopting the same strategies of standardization, consolidation, and automation that are needed for enterprise grid computing.

Summary

This chapter provided a brief history of grid computing from its origins in the scientific community to its current applicability within an enterprise and across partner enterprises. We also provided a glimpse at how we believe "computing as a utility" may look. We presented definitions and terms that you may encounter when dealing with the grid concept. Finally, we presented evidence in terms of technology and business trends that make this concept viable in enterprises today.

The next chapter will describe the standards activities in this space and outline the roadmap for some of these standards.

References

[EGA Roadmap] Accelerating the Adoption of Grid Solutions in the Enterprise. Enterprise Grid Alliance, Dec 2004. http://www
.gridalliance.org/imwp/idms/popups/pop_download.asp?contentid=
2860

[GGF OGSA Glossary] Treadwell, J. (ed.) Open Grid Services Architecture Glossary of Terms. Global Grid Forum OGSA-WG. GFD-I.044, Jan 2005. http://www.ggf.org/documents/GWD-I-E/GFD-I.044.pdf

4

Grid Standards Activities

Many standards organizations are working on different parts of the grid puzzle. These organizations also have liaison relationships among each other to collaborate on related activities. This chapter talks about the efforts of key standards organizations that are driving the standards for technology and processes for grid computing.

Enterprise Grid Alliance (EGA)

The EGA (http://www.gridalliance.org) is a consortium of leading vendors and end users focused on developing enterprise grid solutions and accelerating the deployment of grid computing in the enterprise. It is open, independent, and vendor neutral.

Goals

The overall goal of the EGA is to promote adoption of grid computing within and among organizations. EGA aims to accelerate the use of grid technology in data centers, behind firewalls, and in public and private sector enterprises. The focus of the EGA is to advocate the unique requirements of enterprise data centers and develop standards that address these requirements.

Relevance to Enterprise Grid Computing

EGA is the leading grid consortium that is advocating the requirements of enterprise data centers. As it has laid out in its roadmap, the first phase of the EGA focuses on enterprise grid computing within a single enterprise data center for applications such as CRM and ERP. The goal of the EGA is to address these requirements expeditiously while leveraging existing industry standards if they are available, or by collaborating with standard bodies if in active development. EGA has therefore established liaison relationships with other standard bodies such as GGF, DMTF, and SNIA.

Oracle is a founding member of the EGA and is actively involved in EGA activities. It can be expected that Oracle will leverage the recommendations of EGA in its products.

EGA Roadmap

The EGA has set out a grid development roadmap with three distinct phases, as defined in the EGA document "Accelerating the Adoption of Grid Solutions in the Enterprise" [EGA Roadmap].

Phase I: Core Capability

In its first phase, currently in progress, the EGA is focusing tightly on enterprise grid computing within a single administrative domain. These include enterprise applications such as enterprise resource planning (ERP), customer relationship management (CRM), business intelligence (BI), and enterprise data integration. These applications and systems run behind a firewall in one data center of a single organization. The goal of Phase I work is to provide basic interoperability among grid components from many vendors in a single data center.

Phase II: Include and Extend

In the next phase, the EGA plans to broaden its focus to include a wider variety of application types including technical applications, such as simulation, modeling, and financial portfolio analysis, and to address data and compute-cycle sharing among multiple grids. This will extend the grid to partner organizations and customers, and provide basic interoperation among enterprise grid environments. This work will encompass support of web service calls across applications, scheduling compute-intensive tasks, workflows, etc.

Phase III: Unify and Complete

In this third phase, the grid computing paradigm will be opened up to include cross-entity resource sharing, which may include extending data stores, applications, and compute resources over a dedicated network or over the open Internet. This final phase of development of the grid concept will allow for service provider business models, so any company can purchase IT resources just as they would any other utility. The utility computing model will be enabled by capacity-on-demand, dynamic capacity addition, and complete support for a wide range of enterprise applications.

EGA Working Groups

The EGA is addressing an initial set of identified enterprise requirements in its technical working groups and regional committees. Each working group focuses on specific problem areas within grid computing.

One of the main EGA working groups is the reference model working group, which provides all of the other EGA working groups with a shared context. In May 2005, the reference model working group released the first version of its reference model [EGA Ref Model]. The reference model describes, among other things, how various grid components function in the data center, their relationship to each other, and their life cycles. This document is available for download from the EGA web site: http://www.gridalliance.org.

Other EGA working groups are responsible for defining requirements and use cases for problem areas such as usage accounting, security, component provisioning, and data provisioning.

Global Grid Forum (GGF)

The GGF (http://www.ggf.org) is the premier organization driving the standards for grid computing at large. It is a community-initiated forum of thousands of individuals from industry and research leading the global standardization effort for grid computing.

Goals

Based on an extensive study, GGF refined its mission in February 2005 to "lead the pervasive adoption of grid computing for research and industry" [GGF Oper]. GGF aims to define grid specifications that lead to broadly adopted standards and interoperable software, and build a broad international community for exchange of ideas, experiences, requirements, and best practices.

Relevance to Enterprise Grid Computing

The GGF works on the broad spectrum of grid computing problems and solutions across both research and industry. Its community groups encompass representatives across different industries and scientific and research institutions. GGF has various working groups that are involved in defining GGF standards, liaison strategy, and the GGF roadmap, as well as driving standards and specifications development. For example, the Open Grid Services Architecture (OGSA™) working group defines the overall architecture of the grid and provides structure to other groups that are working on different underlying pieces of the puzzle.

GGF also has liaison relationships with other relevant standards bodies such as IETF, W3C, OASIS, and EGA.

Open Grid Services Architecture (OGSA) v1.0

OGSA is GGF's blueprint for enabling information and resource sharing across departments and among organizations utilizing products from a variety of different vendors. It also serves as an integration point for collaboration among the various standards bodies engaged in delivering on the vision of industry-standard distributed computing.

OGSA v1.0, released in January 2005, is an informational document that provides an architectural framework for grid deployment [GGF OGSA Arch]. This architectural framework is made up of a number of service categories including infrastructure services, execution management services, data services, resource management services, etc. Working groups at GGF in collaboration with other standards bodies are defining standards and specifications for these service categories. A detailed description of the OGSA specification is beyond the scope of this book.

OGSA and underlying standards that it depends on are in active development. Hence, enterprises cannot yet build a grid with OGSA. But the important point to note is that information contained in OGSA v1.0 and other related documents is being used by various standards organizations, open source and packaged software vendors, and end users of grids to ensure that they stay in sync with standardization efforts.

World Wide Web Consortium (W3C)

The W3C (http://www.w3c.org) is an international consortium where member organizations, a full-time staff, and the public work together to develop web standards. W3C's mission is to lead the World Wide Web to its full potential by developing protocols and guidelines that ensure long-term growth for the Web. The World Wide Web Consortium (W3C) develops interoperable technologies (specifications, guidelines, software, and tools) to lead the Web to its full potential.

Relevance to Enterprise Grid Computing

Starting with HTTP, HTML, and URIs, W3C has led the evolution of the Web. One of the long-term goals for the W3C is to make the benefits of the Web available to everyone, make the Web easily accessible from any device, and to make the knowledge base on the Web amenable to human and computer access. W3C is therefore involved in a number of areas, but the two broad areas of interest to the grid community are XML and Web Services.

XML was originally developed at the W3C. The XML core working group continues to develop and maintain the specifications for XML itself and closely related specifications. W3C also is designing the infrastructure and defining the architecture and the core technologies for Web Services. The goal of the Web Services activity is to design a set of technologies that fit in the Web's architecture in order to lead Web Services to their full potential. Web Services provide a standard means of interoperating among different software applications, running on a variety of platforms and/or frameworks.

Web Services Architectural Framework

The Web Services Architectural Framework includes a collection of standards from W3C dealing with various aspects of application design revolving around Service-Oriented Architectures. Figure 4-1 shows how different Web Services technologies from W3C fit together.

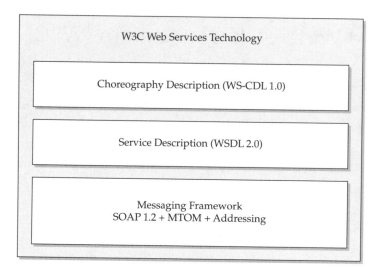

Figure 4.1   *W3C Web Services technologies*

The XML Messaging Framework includes SOAP, which provides an XML-based messaging framework for exchanging XML data through a web interface. WS-Addressing provides the addressing framework for messages between applications, particularly asynchronous interactions. The Web Services Description (WSDL) specifies how to format and include information such as end-point addresses, supported protocols, etc., in a web service message. The Web Services Choreography Description Language (WS-CDL) specifies how to compose and describe the relationships and message exchange between Web Services.

Organization for the Advancement of Structured Information Standards (OASIS)

OASIS (http://www.oasis-open.org) aims to drive the development, convergence, and adoption of e-business standards. OASIS has been one of the primary consortiums driving the standards on Web Services. The consortium also hosts two of the most widely respected information portals on XML and Web Services standards, Cover Pages (http://xml.coverpages.org) and XML.org (http://www.xml.org).

Relevance to Enterprise Grid Computing

OASIS members are defining many of the infrastructure standards that enable Web Services, as well as the implementation standards that are used in specific communities and across industries.

Some of the relevant standards defined by OASIS include Universal Description, Discovery and Integration (UDDI), and Web Services Business Process Execution Language (WSBPEL). UDDI provides a standard method for enterprises to dynamically discover and invoke Web Services. BPEL enables users to describe business process activities as Web Services and define how they can be connected to accomplish specific tasks. OASIS also provides standards to represent management interfaces for Web Services, notification services allowing Web Services to disseminate information to each other, reliable messaging, security of Web Services, and modeling of stateful resources using Web Services.

The reason these Web Services standards from W3C and OASIS are relevant to grid computing is because they enable Service-Oriented Architecture at the application layer, which as we discussed in the earlier chapters, is the foundation of application-layer grid computing. The BPEL standard is especially important because it allows enterprises to define their business processes and process flows in a declarative fashion, rather than hardwiring them into application software code.

Distributed Management Task Force (DMTF)

The DMTF (http://www.dmtf.org) is focused on and has been leading the development of management standards and integration technology for enterprise and Internet environments. DMTF standards provide common management infrastructure components for instrumentation, control, and communication in a platform-independent and technology-neutral way.

Relevance to Enterprise Grid Computing

DMTF is leading the charge for development of standards that enable interoperable data center management solutions and reduce costs of data center management. DMTF standards are relevant to grid computing as they directly aid in enabling and simplifying centralized management of an enterprise grid, i.e., an enterprise data center. DMTF has defined the CIM and WBEM standards for exchange of management information.

The Common Information Model (CIM) is a model for exchange of management information for hardware, software, and services in a platform-independent and technology-neutral way, enabling end-to-end multivendor interoperability in management systems. Web-based Enterprise Management (WBEM) leverages existing Internet and Web Services technologies for the interoperable exchange of management information.

Storage Networking Industry Association (SNIA)

The SNIA (http://www.snia.org) is the consortium driving standards in the storage networking industry. SNIA's mission is to advance the adoption of storage networks as complete and trusted solutions. Its members include storage vendors and customers. SNIA has established itself as an authority for standards in data and storage networks.

Relevance to Enterprise Grid Computing

Initiatives at SNIA help in enabling enterprise grid computing at the storage layer. Two initiatives at SNIA are particularly relevant to the grid community—the Storage Management Initiative (SMI) and the Data Management Forum (DMF).

SMI developed the SMI-S specification, which includes standard interfaces to discover, monitor, and manage storage components. As storage vendors increasingly begin to comply with SMI-S, it will address the problem of implementing and managing multivendor storage infrastructures. The DMF aims to define, implement, qualify, and teach improved and reliable methods for the protection, retention, and lifecycle management of electronic data and information.

What Do the Standards Mean for Your Enterprise?

At this point, you may be wondering how the discussion on standard bodies and standards is relevant to your immediate enterprise grid computing plans. It appears that there is a whole variety of standards under development, and current grid-related technology may or may not incorporate these standards. In fact, we mentioned that standards like OGSA are not ready for incorporation into enterprise grid solutions. Does this mean you should sit on the sidelines and wait for this these standards to mature, or can you get started today?

The IT industry is a fast-moving industry and there will always be new technologies and emerging standards. It is impractical to wait for a technology to stop evolving. Rather, it is important to focus on building solutions using existing standards, and work with established vendors whose technology will evolve to incorporate future standards when they mature and become relevant in the marketplace. For example, the Oracle 10g platform provides the infrastructure for running applications using the Oracle Database and Applications Server in a grid environment today. It does support existing standards like SQL, Java, ODBC, JDBC, Web Services, and many others. In addition, it can be expected to support grid standards such as OGSA when they are ready.

Summary

The point to take away from this chapter is that many people are working on standardizing the technology and process elements of grid computing. Oracle and other established grid vendors are actively participating and collaborating in all these standards bodies. This indicates significant vendor mindshare and agreement on the grid computing concept, and therefore it can be expected that future products will incorporate these standards as they mature. Further, since many of these developing grid standards are for infrastructure, you may be able to take advantage of these standards automatically by simply upgrading your infrastructure software (OS, database, middleware), without any changes to your applications.

In the next and final chapter, we will provide some practical guidance for embarking on a grid computing initiative within your enterprise, as well as some strategic steps for incrementally evolving IT from its current state to an enterprise grid.

References

[EGA Roadmap] Accelerating the Adoption of Grid Solutions in the Enterprise. Enterprise Grid Alliance, Dec 2004. http://www .gridalliance.org/imwp/idms/popups/pop_download.asp?contentid= 2860

[EGA Ref Model] EGA Reference Model v1.0. Enterprise Grid Alliance Reference Model Working Group, May 2005. http:// www .gridalliance.org/en/WorkGroups/ReferenceModel.asp

[GGF Oper] Linesch, Mark. Global Grid Forum – Changes to GGF Operating Model. GGF, GWD-CP, Feb 4th, 2005. http://www.ggf.org/ documents/Global_Grid_Forum_-Changes_to_GGF_Operating_ Model%5B1%5D.doc

[GGF OGSA Arch] Foster, I., Kishimoto, H., Savva, A., Berry, D., Djaoui, A., Grimshaw, A., Horn, B., Maciel, F., Siebenlist, F., Subramaniam, R., Treadwell, J., and Von Reich, J. The Open Grid Services Architecture, Version 1.0. GGF OGSA Working Group (OGSA-WG), Jan 2005. http:// www.ggf.org/documents/GWD-I-E/GFD-I.030.pdf

5

Steps to Grid Adoption

Great! We now understand the enterprise grid computing concept and appreciate its benefits. But how do enterprises adopt grid computing incrementally while leveraging their current IT investments? In this chapter, we provide various practical steps to transition an existing IT infrastructure to an enterprise grid, particularly for Oracle environments.

We start with a discussion on the barriers of transitioning to grid computing and how to overcome them. We then talk about how to identify the first steps to transition to grid computing and how to scale this project over time. Enterprise grid computing can be adopted by enterprises in three strategic steps—standardization, consolidation, and automation. We discuss how enterprise architects and strategists can apply these three tenets to different aspects of the IT lifecycle.

Transitioning to the Grid

Any project that changes the establishment is likely to encounter resistance from different quarters. Enterprise grid computing changes the way IT is currently done in a major way and so an enterprise leader heading this change will face numerous barriers in the form of people, process, and technology. Therefore, careful thought and effort must be put into identifying a pilot project for grid computing. This project should be a sweet spot that clearly demonstrates tangible benefits and substantial ROI to the enterprise. Once success is achieved at this project, the barriers will ease, and over time, the idea and experience gained can be applied to other aspects of IT.

Barriers to Grid Adoption

An enterprise leader driving the transition to enterprise grid computing needs to overcome the resistance of people who are used to doing things the old-fashioned way. There is a lot of hype and confusion surrounding grid computing in general—regarding the concept itself and also the technology, standards, and processes involved. We hope that Chapters 3 and 4 helped clarify some of those issues. Now let us understand some of the common issues one is likely to encounter when starting a grid computing initiative within an enterprise.

Server Hugging

Organizations have a sense of ownership over the resources bought or allocated for their use. They fear that by not having these resources close to them or managed by them, they would lose this control, and might not be able to get access to the resources they need to perform their tasks. They also feel that a grid with shared servers, storage, and data would weaken the data security barriers between different grid users. Application users may be wary of their applications being run at lower priorities or with reduced resources compared to other applications.

These political and organizational barriers are sometimes harder than the technical barriers. It can be difficult to convince these business units to accede to the change. Later in this chapter, we will suggest some steps for how to address these problems.

Unrealistic Expectations from Grid Computing

There is confusion over the reality of grid computing. Marketing departments have run amuck and have marketed the grid "nirvana" and not the grid that exists and is possible today. Not every promise of grid computing can be realized today and the transition to grid cannot be achieved overnight. Unrealistic expectations will most certainly lead to failure and disenchantment. Some of the most common misconceptions resulting from the over-hype of grid computing include these:

- *It is possible to create a grid with a mix of windows boxes, Linux boxes, and Solaris boxes.* While this may be possible, it is fraught with many technical challenges and often does not provide the benefits that organizations are seeking. It is much easier to share resources across applications when they have been standardized on a common platform. For example, when running in a homogeneous environment, you can use Oracle Real Application Clusters to spread your database workload across the servers in your environment.

- *With grid computing, enterprise applications can magically utilize idle desktops and bring them into the grid for computations.* While you could write an application that could possibly send computations to an idle box sitting on your network, you cannot randomly bring a desktop into your grid. Most enterprise applications require a tight coupling between servers hosting the application (unlike many scientific apps). There are other issues, including security, because of which you may not want to use these boxes to run your enterprise application.

- *Service-oriented architecture is the panacea for application integration problems. Wrap all applications with Web Services and these applications can start talking to each other to create dynamic business process networks.* While web service technologies make it easier to expose applications as services to the outside world, all the parties involved do have to come up with a common set of exposed service names, their attributes, and semantics to create dynamic business process networks.

Lack of Grid Standards

Grid standards are in active development and may not be incorporated into products yet. Due to the lack of grid standards, there is limited vendor interoperability, particularly in the area of dynamic and autonomic resource provisioning. However, this should not stop enterprises from adopting the grid computing approach today.

Enterprises can start their grid computing initiative by adopting the grid computing methodology, while leveraging their current investments. Given the direction of Oracle's grid computing technologies, enterprises adopting these technologies will automatically gain additional grid benefits as Oracle incorporates grid standards in its products. Customers using the Oracle platform also do not need to rewrite their applications to gain the grid benefits.

Implementing Change

Implementing change at any organization is a huge undertaking. There are a number of books solely devoted to the topic of implementing change in an organization. Concepts and best-practice models discussed in those books apply equally well for implementing the change brought about by the enterprise grid computing model. The move to enterprise grid computing must make effective use of people, process, and technology. The next few sections discuss various approaches to ease the transition process.

Executive Support for Grid Computing

Transition to grid is similar to the transition from client-server to multitier application models during the Internet boom—it is a continuous process and requires long-term commitment. Therefore, it is important to have executive support for this initiative. A leader with strong resolve can go a long way in convincing different business units to join in the grid effort. This leader can help in addressing the political and organizational issues and in resolving difficult situations that may arise in the transition to enterprise grid computing.

Overcoming Server Hugging

As discussed earlier, one of the barriers to grid is that business units fear the loss of control over their resources. In order to overcome this type of resistance, you must convince business units how the grid can potentially offer them more resources than they currently have. If creating a server grid, identify use cases for these business units where a grid environment can expeditiously address a sudden surge in computing demands that could otherwise have resulted in a downtime. Demonstrate how a new application that took months to deploy in their current environment can be deployed much more quickly with dynamic resource provisioning. If creating an information grid, discuss the value of the consolidated information with the potential business users.

Overcoming "People" Barriers

People tend to resist change because they do not want to step out of their comfort zone—they like to stay in an environment they are comfortable with. Older power structures feel threatened by the change. People who have enjoyed luxury in the old structure feel that new structure will take their power or luxury away. Listed here are some things that can be done to reduce the resistance to this change:

- **Effective communication**   It is important to have a clear and open communication from the management to convey the reason for the change and the overall positive impact the change will have on the organization. Most importantly, people need to know how they will fit in the new organization and business units need to know how their needs will continue to be met in the new model.

- **Team building**   Creating a cohesive cross-organization team builds confidence in the team members, and they are more willing to accept the change as they work towards a common goal. As grid addresses the resource requirements across multiple business units, the administrative resources across those business units can be brought together to accomplish the task of building this grid.

- **Time to adapt**   It takes time for people to get used to the new concept and the new way of computing, so it is imperative that business units are given sufficient time to adjust and get comfortable with enterprise grid computing. As organizations gain experience with the grid model, they need to learn new social behaviors for optimal functioning of the grid. For instance, now business units should not install new software or arbitrary patches on the servers by themselves. They need to ensure that the software version follows the enterprise standards; in addition, they need to get grid administrators to put new patches through better testing before applying them. Business units may resist this effort, claiming it to be too time-consuming or restrictive. It is necessary to convince them that the change towards standardization simplifies configuration management of the systems, and will give them a better handle over troubleshooting software-related issues.

Starting Small

Perhaps the most important factor for success is to start small. Find a sweet spot. IT is constantly evolving. Look for an IT organization that is struggling to address a resource shortage or trying to achieve a specific performance goal, and then see if grid computing can be used to solve the problem. We discuss this topic in greater detail in the next section.

Identifying a Sweet Spot

There is a lot of literature available on the topic of identifying a sweet spot that applies to enterprise grid computing as well. It is very difficult to put the organization through a big change in one big swoop. Start with something that is easy and possesses widespread organizational support, perhaps even where the solution has already been implemented elsewhere.

A sweet spot has the following characteristics:

- It offers the path of least resistance;
- It provides substantial measurable benefits on a small scale; and
- It achieves result within a stipulated time.

There is no fixed sweet spot for entry into the enterprise grid computing. It really depends on the challenges and goals of the enterprise. Here are some examples that may apply to your enterprise:

- If the enterprise is in the cycle of acquiring new hardware resources, look at low-cost modular servers to run Oracle databases (using Real Application Clusters) or to run application servers. Start with one application on the cluster of low-cost servers and incrementally move more applications to this group. Gradually consolidate more databases and application servers on this cluster of low-cost servers.

- If the enterprise is struggling with its inability to scale its IT management staff to meet its growing IT demands, then the place to start enterprise grid computing is to explore centralized management tools. For example, Oracle Grid Control can be used to manage the IT infrastructure for Oracle databases and application servers, as well as for their associated server and OS resources. This will help scale administrators to the growing IT infrastructure.

- If the enterprise has a data-intensive application—like business analytics—that needs additional database resources, offload processing to databases with more server resources by utilizing Oracle Database's data provisioning technologies such as Transportable Tablespaces and Streams. These technologies help in moving data efficiently in bulk to the available database resource.

- If enterprises are looking at modularizing their application development or improving their business process flows, look at Service-Oriented Architectures and service development and deployment technologies from Oracle Application Server. Consider using Oracle BPEL Process Manager to manage the creation and optimization of new workflows among the services.

Scaling Out

Once the benefits of the grid have been demonstrated on a small scale, it is time to scale out and expand the benefits to cover a more substantial part of the enterprise. On the political front, scaling out with enterprise grid computing is very similar to that of any other widespread organizational changes. Make the transition to enterprise grid computing a grassroots effort and build momentum for change among employees. Identify as many of the potential "hot buttons" of your audience (i.e., sponsors, opinion leaders, budget controllers, policy makers, and enforcers, etc.) as possible. Translate the solution to reflect how the change will satisfy each of their needs, especially those regarding cost, quality, and service.

On the technical front, enterprise grid computing is inherently amenable to scaling out. Once you have demonstrated the benefits of grid computing on a smaller group of resources, more resources and more applications can be moved to this grid incrementally. More and more applications can share this group of resources to meet their collective needs.

Once you have centralized the management of a small group of applications, you can add more applications and more data center components to this group. You can manage resources as a group and scale your administrative resources to manage more and more applications.

Once you have created an SOA-based architecture for a smaller group of applications, you can add more application services to this mix and create more dynamic and more powerful business process networks.

Strategic Steps Towards an Enterprise Grid

In this section, we talk about the strategic steps that enterprises can take to set themselves on the long-term path for grid computing. While conducting the strategic planning for the evolution of their IT infrastructure, enterprise strategists should incorporate the tenets of standardization, consolidation, and automation in their plan.

Standardization

Standardizing on technology involves reducing the number of heterogeneous products and vendors—hardware and software. Standardization also applies to the architecture for deployment of these products and for all processes in the IT lifecycle from development, deployment, management, and decommissioning.

Vendor Standardization

Enterprises should standardize on vendors who can deliver them with technology to address their IT needs today and can continue to address their future IT needs. Vendor standardization also provides them with a "single throat to choke" in case of problems. Vendor standardization reduces the variability and the complexity found in the traditional data centers. It can be expected that the products provided by the single vendor interoperate with each other and come with best-practice product deployments. When choosing vendors, preference should be given to those whose products support available industry standards in that space.

Product Standardization

Enterprises should standardize on a small group of products that can be deployed for use throughout their IT. A single product and its deployment configuration can be tested by a centralized IT department before it is approved for general deployments throughout the enterprise. This reduces the amount of resources spent in testing cycles across various IT departments. Centralized testing also ensures that the product goes through more thorough testing. With this standardization, it becomes easier to create interoperable applications and also to possibly consolidate these applications in the future.

As an example, Linux is becoming the platform of choice for low-cost enterprise application deployments, and every major server vendor has a blade server offering. Therefore, blade servers running Linux OS could potentially serve as the standard platform for server deployments in the enterprise.

On the Oracle Database side, enterprises should standardize on a small number of versions that are well-tested and approved for use by various IT departments. Enterprises should also determine a small number of architectural configurations for the Oracle Database. Various departments can then choose from this configuration set, based on their needs. This reduces the variability and provides better testing of and increased confidence in deploying those architectures. Similarly, enterprises should standardize on a smaller number of configurations for their application servers.

Standardization on Standards

Enterprises should standardize on the use of standards, wherever available, for application development. Standards, by nature, have widespread use and widespread vendor support. Applications developed using standards have longer shelf life. It can be expected that the applications developed using industry standards will continue to work on the grid deployments as grid technologies are developed in the future. J2EE and Web Services are the most popular technologies of choice for application development and deployment. The Oracle 10*g* platform supports a variety of industry standards throughout its stack.

Process Standardization

Enterprises should standardize the various processes throughout the lifecycle of enterprise data center components including applications, hardware, software, etc. Process standardization reduces the variability in this lifecycle and reduces chances of errors.

In the selection phase, standardization ensures that only those products that suit the enterprise needs make the cut. In the development and QA phase, process standardization ensures that the repeatable processes are followed for taking the environment from development to QA, and that the product goes through sufficient testing before it can be approved for mass deployment. In the deployment phase, it ensures that the deployed environment is the same as the one that has been approved by QA. In the production phase, it ensures that the repeatable and correct procedures are followed for regular ongoing maintenance of the production environments. In the decommissioning phase, it ensures the component is securely decommissioned, i.e., no confidential information can be stolen from the decommissioned component.

Consolidation

The next step after standardization is consolidation. Enterprises must set up a long-term goal to consolidate all aspects of their IT infrastructure.

In place of having many distributed IT environments, enterprises should reduce the number of data centers to a handful. A consolidated data center brings the benefits of the economy of scale for managing a large number of data center components at one place. In addition to the reduction in overall power, cooling, and space requirements, it substantially reduces the overall management costs of the IT infrastructure.

Consolidate and reduce the number of application servers and the databases. Enterprises do not need to have a separate database and application server for each application. Enterprises could run multiple applications on a single database and a single application server. They should move towards consolidation of the total number of databases they have in their enterprise. Oracle Database and Application Server have capabilities that ensure that the various applications running on them get the appropriate amount of resources to meet their performance needs.

Enterprises should consolidate their hardware infrastructure. On the server side, blade servers can provide the standard hardware platform by consolidating the server infrastructure into racks of blade servers. Technologies available from the blade vendors and Oracle ensure that these blades can be appropriately provisioned for the various enterprise application needs.

On the storage front, SAN and NAS led the wave for consolidation. Technologies from Oracle and storage vendors further help in rationalizing and consolidating the storage environment. These technologies unify their storage infrastructure with an integrated storage architecture that supports NAS, SAN, and IP SAN, and delivers on a range of the quality of service requirements (backup and recovery, HA, performance, etc.) to meet the various application needs.

Enterprises should work towards integrating data scattered throughout different databases within the enterprises. The integration may be physical by moving the data into one database or logical by using products like data hubs. Having a common interface to data for all applications essentially virtualizes the information source from the application, and will ease future migration efforts towards new application architectures, such as ones based on SOA.

Automation

The next step after standardization and consolidation is automation. Standardization and consolidation make it easy to automate various processes involved in the IT lifecycle. Automation reduces the overall cost of IT management. On the soft benefits side, automation significantly reduces risks as it lowers the chances of human error, thus providing a more dependable IT. Enterprise architects should be on the lookout for the various aspects of IT that can be automated in their strategic planning.

Standardized processes are more amenable to automation. Once the processes are standardized and the IT infrastructure is consolidated, scripts and automation tools can be used to automate a good portion of these processes. The job system in the Oracle Grid Control can also help in this process. Scripts can be automated by setting them up as jobs managed by Oracle Grid Control. Jobs can be run on demand or scheduled to run at a specific time or periodically. Enterprises can find elements for automation in every cycle of IT. Some examples include these:

- **Automated Initial Deployment of a Server**   Oracle Grid Control provides bare metal install of a Linux OS and the Oracle software on that server. Certified images of the OS and its patches and the Oracle software can be maintained using Oracle Grid Control.

When a new box is brought in, this new box is automatically configured using Oracle Grid Control with the appropriate software. This ensures that well-tested and certified software is deployed throughout the enterprise.

- **Automated Patching**   Oracle Grid Control can periodically check for any patches that are available for the enterprise's IT environment. If these are available, it notifies administrators. Based on the nature of these patches, administrators can schedule those patches to be applied to the affected systems.

- **Automated Ongoing Maintenance**   Regular maintenance tasks such as taking regular backups, etc., can be automated. If IT systems are set up using a small number of configurations, the same scripts can be run periodically for regular maintenance of those environments. Failures or exceptions during these operations are flagged and administrators are only called in when corrective actions are required.

Summary

Evolution of traditional IT infrastructure towards enterprise grid is a combination of people, process, and technology. Enterprise grid computing affects every aspect of the IT lifecycle. The process for the transition to enterprise grid is very similar to any other big change that needs to be brought about within an organization. Start with a sweet spot and scale it to affect the broader and bigger aspects of IT. The move to enterprise grid computing can be started at any place; that sweet spot can be selected based on the current goals and challenges faced by the enterprise. After achieving success by realizing the goals on the small-scale project, the grid can be scaled out to include more applications and more business units. As the grid computing technologies are inherently amenable to scale out, these technologies simplify this step.

Enterprises can gradually evolve towards grid computing by pursuing a strategy of standardization, consolidation, and automation throughout the IT lifecycle. Standardization refers to standardization at every layer of IT: a) servers using low-cost modular servers, b) software stack, c) enterprise deployment architectures, d) use of standards, and e) process. Consolidation also applies to several areas: a) data centers, b) databases and application servers, and c) servers and storage information. Automation refers to automation of processes and IT management tasks.

Enterprise grid computing has something to offer for every enterprise. Starting with small steps today, you can be on the path to a full-fledged enterprise grid that can constantly evolve and provide increasing benefits to the business.

INDEX